DEVELOPING LITERACY

Photocopiable teaching resources for

UNDERSTANDING AND RESPONDING TO TEXTS

Ages 10–11

Christine Moorcroft

& C Black • London

Published 2008 by A & C Black Publishers Limited
38 Soho Square, London W1D 3HB
www.acblack.com

ISBN 978-0-7136-8465-0

Copyright text © Christine Moorcroft 2008
Copyright illustrations © Kevin Hopgood 2008
Copyright cover illustration © Piers Baker 2008
Editor: Jane Klima
Designed by Susan McIntyre

The author and publishers would like to thank Ray Barker and Rifat Siddiqui for their
advice in producing this series of books.

A CIP catalogue record for this book is available from the British Library.

The author and publishers are grateful for permission to reproduce the following:

p.14: From *The Lion, the Witch and the Wardrobe* by C. S. Lewis. Reproduced by
permission of The C. S. Lewis Company Ltd. p.15: From *The Haunting* by Margaret
Mahy. Reproduced by permission of Egmont UK. p.16: From *The Edge Chronicles:
Beyond the Deepwoods* by Paul Stewart and Chris Riddell. Reproduced by
permission of Random House. p.25: From *Skellig* by David Almond. Reproduced by
permission of Hachette Children's. From *Said and Done* by Roger McGough.
Reproduced by permission of Random House. p.58: 'Mushrooms' by Sylvia Plath.
Reproduced by permission of Faber and Faber. p.62: 'Take One Home For The
Kiddies' by Philip Larkin. Reproduced by permission of Faber and Faber. Every effort
has been made to trace copyright holders and to obtain their permission for use of
copyright material. The authors and publishers would be pleased to rectify any error
or omission in future editions.

Printed by Halstan Printing Group, Amersham, Buckinghamshire.

A&C Black uses paper produced with ele███████lorine-free pulp, harvested from
managed sustainable forests.

Contents

Introduction

100% New Developing Literacy Understanding and Responding to Texts is a series of seven photocopiable activity books for developing children's responses to different types of text and their understanding of the structure and purposes of different types of text.

The books provide learning activities to support strands 7 and 8 (Understanding and interpreting texts and Engaging with and responding to texts) of the literacy objectives of the Primary Framework for Literacy and Mathematics.

The structure of *100% New Developing Literacy Understanding and Responding to Texts: Ages 10–11* complements the objectives of the Primary Framework and includes the range of text types suggested in the planning for children aged 10–11. It focuses on the following types of text:

- Narrative (Fiction genres, Extending narrative, Authors and texts, Short stories with flashbacks)
- Non-fiction (Biography and autobiography, Journalistic writing, Argument, Formal/impersonal writing)
- Poetry (The power of imagery, Finding a voice).

100% New Developing Literacy Understanding and Responding to Texts: Ages 10–11 addresses the following learning objectives from the Primary Framework for Literacy:

Strand 7 Understanding and interpreting texts

- Appraise a text quickly, deciding on its value, quality or usefulness
- Understand underlying themes, causes and points of view
- Understand how writers use different structures to create coherence and impact
- Explore how word meanings change when used in different contexts
- Recognise rhetorical devices used to argue, persuade, mislead and sway the reader.

Strand 8 Engaging with and responding to texts

- Read extensively and discussing personal reading with others, including in reading groups
- Sustain engagement with longer texts, using different techniques to make the text come alive
- Compare how writers from different times and places present experiences and use language.

The activities

Some of the activities can be carried out with the whole class, some are more suitable for small groups and others are for individual work. It is important that the children are encouraged to enjoy novels, stories, plays, films and poetry – not just to learn about how they are written – and that they have opportunities to listen to, repeat, learn, recite, join in and improvise on poems for enjoyment. Many of the activities can be adapted for use at different levels, to suit the differing levels of attainment of the children; several can be used in different ways (see the *Notes on the activities* on page 6). Some activities have been based on specific texts; others are generic. Some of those based on specific texts can be adapted for use with others. Passages from fiction have been selected to act as 'tasters' to encourage the children to read the rest of the book and others by the same author.

Reading

Most children will be able to carry out the activities independently but a few might need help in reading some of the instructions on the sheets. It is expected that someone will read them to or with them, or explain them, if necessary.

Organisation

The activities require very few resources besides pencils, crayons, scissors and glue. Other materials are specified in the Teachers' notes on the pages: for example, fiction, poetry or information books, websites and CD-ROMs.

Extension activities

Most of the activity sheets end with a challenge (*Now try this!*) which reinforces and extends the children's learning. These more challenging activities might be appropriate for only a few children; it is not expected that the whole class should complete them, although many more

NOW TRY THIS!

children might benefit from them with appropriate assistance – possibly as a guided or shared activity. On some pages there is space for the children to complete the extension activities, but others will require a notebook or a separate sheet of paper.

Accompanying CD

The enclosed CD-ROM contains all the activity sheets from the book and allows you to edit them for printing or saving. This means that modifications can be made to differentiate the activities further to suit individual pupils' needs. See page 13 for more details.

Notes on the activities

The notes below expand upon those provided at the bottom of the activity pages. They give ideas for making the most of the activity sheet, including suggestions for the whole-class introduction, the plenary session or for follow-up work using an adapted version of the sheet. To help teachers to select appropriate learning experiences for their pupils, the activities are grouped into sections but the pages need not be presented in the order in which they appear unless stated otherwise.

Stories and poems featured or suggested in this book and supplementary texts

Fiction genres

Adventure:
The Oxford Book of Adventure Stories (ed. Joseph Bristow, OUP), *Fearless* (Tim Lott, Walker), *Fight Game* (Kate Wild, Blackwell), *Oranges in No Man's Land* (Elizabeth Laird, Macmillan), *The Lion, the Witch and the Wardrobe* (C. S. Lewis, Collins), *Framed* (Frank Cottrell Boyce, Macmillan), *Kidnapped* (Robert Louis Stevenson, Penguin Popular Classics), *Treasure Island* (Robert Louis Stevenson, Penguin Popular Classics), *Swallows and Amazons* (Arthur Ransome, Red Fox)

Mystery:
The Haunting (Margaret Mahy, Puffin), *Skellig* (David Almond, Hodder), *Kit's Wilderness* (David Almond, Hodder), *The Edge Chronicles* (Paul Stewart & Chris Riddell, Corgi)

Historical:
Tom's War (Robert Leeson, Puffin), *Power and Stone* (Alice Leader, Puffin), *Goodnight Mister Tom* (Michelle Magorian, Puffin), *The Saga of Erik the Viking* (Michael Foreman, Puffin), *Carrie's War* (Nina Bawden, Puffin), *Out of the Shadow* (Margaret Nash, A & C Black), *Eagle of the Ninth* (Rosemary Sutcliffe, Puffin), *Smith* (Leon Garfield, Puffin)

Quest:
Watership Down (Richard Adams, Puffin), *Northern Lights* (Philip Pullman, Scholastic Point), *The Hobbit* (J. R. R. Tolkien, HarperCollins), *The Mouse and his Child* (Russell Hoban, Faber)

Parody:
Twinkle, Twinkle Little Bat (Lewis Carroll, Macmillan)

Poetry
The Works (chosen by Paul Cookson, Macmillan), *The Works 2* (chosen by Brian Moses & Pie Corbett, Macmillan), *I Like This Poem* (chosen by Kaye Webb, Puffin), *The Hutchinson Treasury of Children's Poetry* (edited by Alison Sage, Hutchinson), *The Kingfisher Book of Children's Poetry* (selected by Michael Rosen, Kingfisher), *The Puffin Book of Twentieth-Century Children's Verse* (edited by Brian Patten, Puffin), *The Poetry Book: Poems for Children* (chosen by Fiona Waters, Dolphin), *Read Me: A Poem A Day For The National Year Of Reading* and *Read Me 2: A Poem For Every Day of The Year* (chosen by Gaby Morgan, Macmillan), *Classic Poems to Read Aloud* (selected by James Berry, Kingfisher), *The Oxford Treasury of Classic Poems* (OUP)

Useful websites
www.bibliomania.com
www.fablevision.com
www.literature.org
www.storiesfromtheweb.org

Narrative
http://www.cool-reads.co.uk/ (reviews by 10–15-year-olds)
http://www.literacytrust.org.uk/links/.html
http://www.kingston.gov.uk/browse/leisure/libraries/childrens_library_service/dual_language.htm (dual-language books)

Selected fiction and non-fiction books and book boxes:
http://www.badger-publishing.co.uk/
http://www.madeleinelindley.com/aboutus.aspx

The Piano by Aidan Gibbons:
For links using IWB software see the Primary Framework. The following work without IWB software:
http://www.gutenberg.org/dirs/etext99/rlwyc10.txt
http://video.google.com/videoplay?docid=5422822544003533526

Film:
www.bfi.org.uk/education/teaching/primary.html (link to BFI and other sites for free material)
www.britfilms.tv
www.bbcmotiongallery.com
www.britishpathe.com
www.video.google.co.uk

Non-fiction
Biography and autobiography
A good source of biographies is football team websites.

John Lennon:
http://www.johnlennon.com/html/biography.aspx (official site)
http://www.beatlesstory.com/page.asp?key=37 (the Beatles Story museum in Liverpool – a reliable source)
Roger McGough:
http://www.rogermcgough.org.uk/ (official site)
http://www.contemporarywriters.com/authors/?p=auth202

Journalistic writing
http://www.bbc.co.uk/radio4/gfi/?focuswin (Radio 4 children's magazine programme – listen online)
http://www.newsademic.com/ (children's newspapers)
http://news.bbc.co.uk/cbbcnews/hi/uk/default.stm

Argument
Mobile phones:
http://info.cancerresearchuk.org/healthyliving/cancercontroversies/mobilephones/
http://news.bbc.co.uk/1/hi/health/4196762.stm
http://news.bbc.co.uk/1/hi/health/4672657.stm
http://www.racfoundation.org/index.php?option=com_content&task=view&id=295&Itemid=35
http://www.cellular-news.com/story/27539.php

Poetry

Classic texts online:
http://www.gutenberg.org/wiki/Main_Page
http://www.bartleby.com/

Poems online:
http://www.poetry-online.org/ (includes a children's section)
http://www.poetryarchive.org/poetryarchive/home.do (famous poets reading their work)

This book is divided into three main sections: **Narrative**, **Non-fiction** and **Poetry**. These are sub-divided to match the Planning Units of the Primary Framework for Literacy.

Narrative

Fiction genres

The activities in this section focus on adventure, mystery and parody. It is assumed that teachers will first review the children's understanding of different genres through sorting books according to genre. Allocate books from the class library to different groups to sort into 'genre' sets, according to the children's own criteria. They might find that some fit into more than one genre: for example, a historical story might also be an adventure, legend or mystery. In this section, wherever an activity includes a long or difficult passage, encourage the children to annotate the text as they focus on particular questions or features.

Adventure story structure (page 14) develops an appreciation of the organisation of adventure stories. The format focuses on the opening of the story, the trigger for the adventure, then the main events and their settings and then the ending. The flow-chart helps the children to consider how the different stages of the story are linked – how one event leads to another – with the help of clues from the pirates. Ask about the effectiveness of their chosen adventure story. Did the structure work well? How well did the opening work, and did it include lots of description or a focus on action/the trigger for the adventure?

The language of adventure (page 15) focuses on analysing the language used in adventure stories to add excitement. The following words are significant: (verbs/verb phrases) *start, scattering, make a dash, rushed, snapping and snarling, stood up on end, howl, plunge, tugging and pulling, flaming*; (adjectives/adjective phrases) *dreadful, as white as paper, huge, snapping, wide open, angry, horrible, confused, like something in a nightmare, neither alive nor dead, bared, tired all over*; (nouns/noun phrases) *a huge grey beast, snapping teeth, a slash of his sword, brute, nightmare, a horrible, confused moment, monster, blood and heat and hair*. The children could also comment on how adverbs are used to modify adjectives, on the use of adverbs and adverb phrases to heighten the effect of verbs, on the way in which comparisons and similes add to adjectives, and on the effect of connectives on the pace of the passage.

Mystery (page 16) is designed to develop the children's appreciation of the organisation of a mystery story. This opening uses flashbacks to tell the reader how the appearance of the ghost is linked with events in Barney's past. The action starts immediately with details about the character and setting emerging during the narrative. The children could compare this with the openings of other mystery stories which begin with a description of the main character and the setting and build up the mystery gradually. Draw attention to the different ways in which authors give the reader these details. See page 6 for other examples of mystery stories.

A tale with tension: 1 and **2** (pages 17–18) help the children to analyse the build-up of tension in a passage. Let them first discuss the criteria for each level of tension. They could use similar graphs (possibly created using computer software) to analyse and compare other passages in the story and in other books or throughout an entire book. Ask them to look for a pattern: for example, tension building up towards the end of a chapter. Compare the children's graphs and discuss any differences. This activity could also provide opportunities for speaking and listening/drama: using drama techniques to explore the build-up of tension.

Parody (page 19) provides a narrative poem that parodies 'The Owl and the Pussycat', which the children will probably have read or heard. If not, it can be found online at http://www.flippyscatpage.com/owlpussycat.html. Ask them to read the original and the parody and to compare the rhythm, the rhyme pattern and the theme and main events. They should notice what has been changed and the mood of the new poem (humorous – as in many parodies).

Extending narrative

In these activities the children explore non-linear quest-type adventure stories to identify the devices authors use to capture the reader's interest as well as identifying language and organisational features. This prepares them for later work on writing similar types of story.

The quest and **Quest choice** (pages 20–21) help the children to consider the choices a character might have at different points in a story and how a character's choices affect the outcome of an adventure story. Other stories involving a quest include, at a simple level, *Puss in Boots* and *The Wizard of Oz*. More complex examples are *The Lion, the Witch and the Wardrobe* by C. S. Lewis and *Parvana's Journey* by Deborah Ellis (set in the Afghan War – see *100% New Developing Literacy Understanding and Responding to Texts: Ages 9–10*). The children could also talk about their own quests: for example, targets they have set out to achieve and the tasks they have to accomplish along the way. They could talk in pairs and report back to the class, highlighting their partner's achievement (making notes when listening for a sustained period).

World to world (page 22) helps the children to understand a feature of adventure stories in which a character can move from one 'world' to another. They learn to recognise the devices authors use to move a character between 'worlds': for example, a doorway, a rabbit-hole, a looking glass, a picture, a wardrobe or cupboard, a time machine or an invisible opening in the atmosphere. They could also use drama techniques to explore these movements – their effect on a character's behaviour and the responses of other characters.

Adventure cards: 1 and **2** (pages 23–24) develop an appreciation of how the different aspects of an adventure story are interlinked. They might prefer to have realistic life-like characters in a realistic life-like setting who move to another setting as they pursue a quest or have fantastical characters meet the life-like ones in an everyday or fantasy setting – they can choose various combinations. Before they begin it is useful to consider the quest-type adventures they have read and to discuss the categories the quests fall into: revenge, righting a wrong, preventing evil or finding an object or person.

Authors and texts

This section develops the children's use of reading journals by encouraging them to give their journal a sharper focus: how the author introduces characters, settings and events. They also explore the stories through drama and mime.

Reading *Skellig*: 1 and **2** (pages 25–26) explore the use of a reading journal through the example of *Skellig* by David Almond. The children develop their skills in using a reading journal so that it can later help them in their own writing. The story begins with a mystery and then uses flashbacks to reveal the main character, his feelings about what is happening within his family, the setting and some details about the recent past. It is important to draw the children's attention to the way in which the author tells a lot about the character and his family and what has been happening to them as well as creating the atmosphere of mystery and introducing the mystery character (Skellig) in seven short paragraphs. Note the way in which the boy as narrator describes the new house: the words express his dismay at the idea of moving and his dislike of the house: the garage *was more like a demolition site or a rubbish dump*; the estate agent *had a stupid grin on his face*, the boy *just wanted him to shut up*.

Character conflicts in *Skellig* (page 27) helps the children to explore conflicts between characters. This format could be adapted for exploring these conflicts between characters in other books and thus to develop a deeper understanding of the story. The children could also explore the changing relationship between two characters: for example, in *Skellig*, Michael is unwilling to make friends with Mina, partly because he misses being able to see his school friends after school and partly because she is a girl, but they discover shared interests and she finds a way of helping Skellig with him. This offers opportunities

for links with work in citizenship on relationships and conflict (making choices and living in a diverse world).

Themes in *Skellig* (page 28) develops the children's appreciation of the use of a reading journal by focusing on an aspect of a book – the different themes running through it. The passage on page 25 (the opening of the book) is likely to have inspired them to read the rest of the book to find out who the mystery man in the garage was, what happened to him and how this affected Michael. Throughout the story Michael expresses his hostility to the move to a new house and is worried about his baby sister, who is ill; through Mina's interest he becomes interested in birds and learns about their anatomy, especially their wing structure, which he links with his developing knowledge of angels – again inspired by Mina, who has become interested in them through her learning about William Blake. They discover that the man in the garage (Skellig) has wings and is an angel; they also know that he has a close affinity with birds (the owls nesting around the old house feed him).

Short stories with flashbacks

This section presents a progression from the activities for 9–10 year olds which explored the use of the camera in the short film *The Piano* by Aidan Gibbons. The film can be found under Resources for Year 5 (Narrative, Unit 5, *The Piano*, by Aidan Gibbons) at http://www.standards.dfes.gov.uk/primaryframe works/library/Literacy/ict/ictks2/. The activities develop the children's ability to express views on how an author uses various techniques to indicate moods in a text or film and to indicate shifts in time between past and present. The focus is on the use of flashbacks presented using film techniques. There are links with speaking and listening/drama: considering the overall impact of a recorded performance; identifying dramatic ways of conveying characters' ideas and feelings; improvising using a range of drama strategies.

The Piano: themes (page 29) explores the themes running through the short film *The Piano* by Aidan Gibbons (see *Useful websites* on page 6). For a more challenging activity, mask the list of possible themes so that the children can identify some for themselves. For a reduced challenge mask those which are not relevant (hatred, money and slavery) so that the children know which ones they are looking for, and model how to find evidence of each theme.

The Piano: music pace graph (page 30) helps the children to appreciate how the film-maker uses music to create the mood of the film and to change it at different points. The focus is on the pace of the music. This could be linked with work in music lessons on pace and rhythm in music. The children could listen to extracts from other pieces of music and collect pictures which match the mood they create. They could also watch other film extracts in order to make simple observations of changes of pace in music. Older short cartoons: for example, *Tom and Jerry*, feature lots of chase sequences and could be a good focus, or you could try filmed versions of novels which the children already know. During the plenary session, show the film again on the interactive whiteboard and stop at different points to discuss what the children feel is happening and what they feel about the pace of the music.

The Piano: **time links** (page 31) develops an understanding of how changes from past to present can be suggested using visual effects such as gestures, camera panning, image-editing and costume. This builds awareness of a flashback or a return to the present.

The Piano: **memories** (page 32) helps the children to identify the roles of different characters in order to prepare a different version of the film. They could draw and make notes on a storyboard to show the scenes they might use when telling the story through the eyes of the other characters (perhaps these could play the piano, with the man and other characters joining and leaving at appropriate points). The children could also write a script for the story and enact it as a mime or with dialogue. Link this with work in drama and with the next section of this book (*Biography and autobiography*). Another possibility is using a pianist (or player of another instrument) playing a piece of music (it could be the one from this film) to link episodes from a biography, perhaps beginning by identifying the three most important people in that person's life and three key events.

Non-fiction
Biography and autobiography

These activities combine narrative with non fiction. They help the children to distinguish between biography and autobiography, to recognise the effect on the reader of the first or third person, and to distinguish between fact and opinion and explicit and implicit points of view. They also analyse the structure and language styles of biographies and autobiographies and develop their own research skills to prepare for writing a biography.

Brief biography: 1 and **2** (pages 33–34) develop an understanding of biography and their ability to extract and interpret information from different biographical sources. This is an opportunity to examine the language and structure of a biography: third person, past tense, time connectives, chronological order. Ask the children to consider any conflicting information, to check it in other sources and to assess the reliability of different sources: for example, the official John Lennon website (see page 6).

Different versions (page 35) develops skills in evaluating the reliability and usefulness of biographical information from different sources, including evidence of bias, through identifying facts and opinions in sections of biographies of the same person. This could be linked with work in history on Henry VIII and could be useful in developing speaking and listening skills if the children

have a chance to discuss why Henry VIII married six times and whether he treated any of his wives fairly. In these biographies the children can find explicit opinions as well as implicit ones (implied through the words and phrases used, such as *got rid of*).

Poetic autobiography: 1 and **2** (pages 36–37) develop an appreciation of the differences between a biography and an autobiography. The children should notice that an autobiography can present details that a biographer would not know: memories and the subject's thoughts and musings about them. Here Roger McGough seems to talk to the reader; he addresses the reader directly: *All right, I was kidding about the kidnap*. The writer invites his readers to fit together the jigsaw of memories he offers – and gives them plenty of help to do so. Point out the words *I wish I could remember*, which show that the parts that follow are drawn from other people's memories: the children should enter these in the 'We remember' speech bubble. 'I learned later' refers to things which Roger McGough did not know at the time, but found out later – and which helped him to understand the situation: the background details in the last two sentences of the text. These activities naturally link with work in poetry – the children might be able to find similarities between Roger McGough's poetic and autobiographical styles: for example, writing in the first person, playing with ideas and words and looking for humour in everyday situations and ideas.

Is this your life? (page 38) provides a format to help the children to research a person's life in preparation for compiling a reasoned account to present orally. They begin with what they already know and what this makes them want to find out: facts about the person, his or her talents, personal qualities, interests and opinions. Emphasise the importance of noting the source of any information so that it can be returned to later, if necessary.

Journalistic writing

This section is about commenting critically on the language style of journalistic writing. The activities involve newspaper, magazine, radio, television and Internet journalism. You could link this work with citizenship (In the media – what's the news?) or geography (What's in the news?) and draw on it to develop speaking and listening skills (using the techniques of dialogic talk to explore ideas, topics or issues, considering examples of conflicts and resolution, exploring the language used).

In the newspaper: 1 and **2** (pages 39–40) present a range of newspaper texts: recount, non-chronological report, advertisement, notice/announcement, argument/comment, horoscope and competition. In identifying the text type the children notice detailed features of the type of language used: tense, person, type of sentence (statement, command, question, exclamation), verb voice (active/passive), connectives (simple/linking, time, cause/reason, purpose), how personal the language is and the level of formality. They could compare the styles and comment on what makes each suitable for the purpose of the text: this can depend on the expected audience, the subject matter and whether a reply is wanted from the audience.

The five Ws (page 41) develops the children's appreciation of the structure of news reports: they should answer the 'five W' questions *Who? What? Where? When?* and *Why?* (They might also answer the question *How?*) In this case the answers are The Chouetts; the closure of their sweet shop; in Demerara Street (the children might wonder where that is, but point out that in local newspapers, the readers will know that it is in their region unless specified otherwise); Friday, 4 June (the children might wonder in which year, but in a news report which does not specify the year it is assumed that the current year is meant); because sales have dropped.

The same but different (page 42) develops an appreciation of the power and potential of communication media and an ability to recognise features of their structure and language. After the children have identified and commented on the facts and opinions presented in each story, ask if they think people are influenced by newspapers. Point out that many people read only one newspaper and so read only one version of the news: if this is biased they might be persuaded to take the point of view of the writer.

Radio news (page 43) develops the children's appreciation of the power and potential of communication media and their ability to recognise features of their structure and language. They listen attentively to an aural news report, make notes for specific purposes, and begin to understand some key features of the structure of radio news programmes and how the presentation is designed to inform and engage audiences. Choose news reports that end with a summary or other comment (for example, a comment about what might happen next). Also play a report that is introduced by a news 'anchor', who thanks the reporter afterwards. Discuss the roles of each of them. Draw out that, like a newspaper, a radio news programme introduces stories through a series of headlines. There might be one or more presenters reading the general news, weather, business and other types of news; there might be interviews with other reporters, experts or members of the public. News items are strictly timed; this limits the amount of information that can be given; space limits the amount of text allowed for a newspaper story, but newspaper readers can spend as long as they need to read each story.

Television news (page 44) develops an appreciation of the power and potential of communication media and an ability to recognise features of their structure and language. Choose news reports that end with a summary or other comment (for example, a comment about what might happen next). Also show a report that is introduced by a news 'anchor', who thanks the reporter afterwards. Discuss the roles of each of them. The children learn that, like a newspaper or a radio news programme, a television news programme introduces stories through a series of headlines. There might be one or more presenters, interviews with other reporters, experts or members of the public and film footage.

News items are strictly timed; this limits the amount of information that can be given; space limits the amount of text allowed for a newspaper story, although newspaper readers can spend as long as they need to read each story.

Different stations (page 45) develops the children's appreciation of the power and potential of communication media and their ability to recognise features of their structure and language. They listen attentively to an aural news report and make notes for specific purposes and begin to understand some key features of the structure of radio news programmes and how they inform and engage audiences. This activity focuses on the ways in which the language and structure of programmes are tailored to different audiences.

The whole programme (page 46) broadens the children's experience to cover a range of news reporting in different media and encourages them to evaluate how the news is presented. It provides a format to help them to focus on different aspects of television news presentation: the role of the presenters and how the studio is organised; how studio reports are linked to one another and to outside reports from different locations and by different reporters and how studio graphics are used. They could discuss the target audience for the different programmes, and how this might influence the features they have noted.

Argument

These activities support work on exploring controversial issues and discussing texts that offer either balanced or biased views. The children identify key language features and explore the structures of arguments in print or other media. There are opportunities for developing speaking and listening skills (using a range of oral techniques to present a persuasive argument, listening to analyse how speakers present points effectively through use of language (and gesture), making notes when listening for a sustained period and discussing how note-taking varies depending on context and purpose).

For, against or balanced (page 47) focuses on identifying bias in arguments. The children learn to recognise the distinction between the persuasive presentation of a point of view and the discursive presentation of a balanced argument.

Audience and purpose: 1 and **2** (pages 48–49) help the children to identify the ways in which an argument can be tailored for presentation to different audiences, depending on the age, interests and subject knowledge of the audience. It also helps them to identify when formal and informal language are appropriate. They learn to recognise and adapt features such as formality of language and personal/impersonal language and vocabulary by noticing details such as person, passive/active verbs, sentence type and structure and vocabulary level (including use of technical or subject vocabulary). The children should annotate the texts to highlight the features that suggest target audience. They could also think about how the final resentation of each text would give clues about audience, too: for example, colours, size of print, design.

Mobile phones – good or bad? (page 50) helps the children to identify the points that support arguments for and against an issue. This can be used to prepare for presenting or writing a balanced argument. The children should weigh the points they have made against one another to check whether the argument they are preparing is balanced. Ask them if they think it is enough to count the points made on each side of the argument and draw out that some points might carry more weight than others: for example, they might think that the facility for parents to be able to know where their children are is more important than the cost or that it outweighs the risk of children being attacked and having phones stolen. The children could develop speaking and listening skills by participating in a whole class debate. (For websites on this topic, see page 6.)

Formal/impersonal writing

This section is about the use of official language in formal situations and identifying the characteristic features of this language style. The children develop an understanding of the differences between standard English in different contexts.

In agreement (page 51) helps the children to distinguish between official and everyday language and to identify the precise differences between them. It is useful to point out that official language has become less formal than it once was: it is now common for the first and second person to be used, for questions to be included and for the language to be made as simple as possible. Explain why the language of a legal agreement, such as a mobile phone agreement, is expressed in more formal language than would be used in conversation; it has to be precise and unambiguous.

Informally (page 52) is about the vocabulary of formal language. If possible, provide a thesaurus that gives separate informal and formal alternatives for words. The children might also be able to distinguish levels of informal vocabulary: for example, vocabulary they use with their friends, with their families, in the classroom and in informal writing. Encourage them to practise and enjoy the language by taking turns at making simple everyday requests using some of the formal terms: for example, 'When will break time commence?'

Site guides (page 53) develops the children's understanding of how non-fiction information can be presented in different formats and media and helps them to evaluate the effectiveness of presentational effects. They also develop their ICT skills as they navigate a website. Note that paper-based documents such as leaflets can go out of date quickly, but websites can be updated. A disadvantage of the Internet, however, is that out-of-date websites frequently remain online. You could combine this with work in citizenship (respect for property, developing our school grounds) and geography (connecting ourselves to the world).

At the lead mines (page 54) develops the children's skills in researching information from an electronic source by asking questions, scanning an electronic text to locate the answers and making notes that can be returned to later to inform their writing. They develop their ICT skills as they navigate the website. This work could be linked with work in geography on mountain environments (Killhope lead mines are located in the Pennines).

Virtual tour (page 55) develops skills in evaluating the effectiveness of a virtual tour. The choice of place could be linked to a planned/completed visit or related to a current topic. The children could compare this with the effectiveness of print-based sources and discuss the advantages of each.

Poetry
The power of imagery

Here the children explore personification in poems. The poems selected as examples provide powerful imagery which is more sophisticated than the imagery they will have encountered in earlier work. They learn how poets use personification to communicate with a reader or listener.

City Jungle: 1 and **2** (pages 56–57) develop an appreciation of how personification can create an image of a place. In 'City Jungle', Pie Corbett uses the connotations of words to create a sinister, menacing effect: *Lizard cars, radiators grin, hunched houses, A motorbike snarls, Streetlights bare their yellow teeth, the motorway's cat-black tongue*. To demonstrate the power of this imagery the children could try writing personified descriptions of places which sound friendly and inviting. This could be linked with informal/impersonal writing about a place: as a follow-up activity they could make notes of imagery to communicate an image of the place they have researched and perhaps visited. Answers for the extension activity might include: spotlights stare, cars snarl, streetlights wink, branches grasp, roots cling. **City Jungle: 2** helps the children to explore the imagery of the poem using drama. They plan how to enact the roles of the personified objects: cars, shop doorways, houses and so on. This will involve discussion about the effect suggested by each image: for example, a shop doorway with its mouth closed. They might enact this by standing still with arms folded, mouth clamped shut and a frowning expression. Let them experiment to find the most appropriate way of enacting each image. They could use a digital camera to photograph one another and then discuss the effects and reread the poem to evaluate how well they portray it.

Mushrooms: 1 and **2** (pages 58–59) develop an appreciation of how personification can create an image of an event using surreal and surprising imagery. 'Mushrooms' uses imagery to present the overnight emergence of the mushrooms as a faceless, powerful army quietly taking over in a silent but sinister way so that no one notices until they 'inherit the earth'. After reading the poem with the children, give them time to talk about the mushrooms and the feelings the poem evokes. After they have chosen the words that best describe them they could describe the picture the poem creates and the atmosphere of the scene. To make the activity more accessible to lower-attaining children you could also ask them to underline any words that describe the mushrooms as if they are people: toes, noses, fists and so on. They might notice how the imagery is enhanced by alliteration and assonance: *toes/noses, soft fists insist, heaving the needles, our hammers, our rams, shoulder through holes, nudgers and shovers*. In the extension activity, the children could develop the idea of the mushrooms as hostile troops, or they might liken the mushrooms to aliens overrunning the planet or bandits springing up in the surrounding hills to lay siege to a town. **Mushrooms: 2** helps them to explore the imagery of the poem through planning a story based on it. This could be a mystery or science fiction story.

Personify this (page 60) encourages the children to create imagery to prepare for writing a poem using what they have learned about personification from the poems on the previous pages.

Finding a voice

> These activities explore how poets express thoughts and feelings about issues; how they use imagery, language and the structure of poems to communicate with readers and listeners.

Cynddylan before and after (page 61) explores how the poet communicates a message. The description of the man on the tractor conjures up pride and power: the man who was once *yoked* to the soil is now in charge of a powerful machine – no longer a slave but a king. The children are encouraged to explore the description on a deeper level: for example, *yoked him to the soil* could mean that he had a strong link with nature, whereas now the birds sing with their *bills wide in vain* and he empties the wood of *foxes and squirrels and bright jays* – he has power but he is no longer part of nature. You could ask the children to look for imagery that suggests that he is now machine-like (*part of the machine, nerves of metal, his blood oil*). They could discuss the effects of technology on people's lives and on their connection to nature to prepare for writing their own poems about another aspect of this: for example, computers, mobile phones, cars, television.

What's the issue? (page 62) encourages the children to explore the way in which the poet expresses thoughts and feelings about living things being treated as playthings. The light-hearted rhythm helps to communicate the levity of the attitude of the children and their parents who buy living things as if they were toys. The negative language (*shadeless; No dark, no dam, no earth, no grass*) evokes the readers' compassion for animals taken from their natural habitat, from their mothers and all comfort to be treated as toys and then discarded. It could be read in connection with work in citizenship (Animals and us) in which the children consider how animals should be treated and the responsibilities people have for their pets.

The hurt boy (page 63) develops an appreciation of how writers use poetry as a powerful means of communicating their thoughts about an issue. It presents a poem that communicates the feelings of despair, anguish, and loneliness of a boy who is bullied. It uses powerful imagery *the crumbs of his heart, made his face a bruised moon, his spectacles stamped to ruin*. The children might be able to identify with the way in which the boy finds comfort and hope through talking to the birds: *Their feathers gave him welcome, Their wings taught him new ways to become* – it is as if he has risen above the bullying. Ask them how the mood of the poem changes at the end and which words communicate this. Suggested answers: sorrow – *fed them the crumbs of his heart*; fear – *things that nightly hissed / as if his pillow was a hideaway for creepy-crawlies*; hurt – *his spectacles stamped to ruin*; pain – *his face a bruised moon*; humiliation – *the note sent to the girl he fancied / held in high mockery*; misery – *secrets he hid under his skin*; loneliness – *The hurt boy talked to the birds*; hope – *taught him new ways to become*; comfort – *gave him welcome*. This poem could be linked with work in citizenship on Choices and Living in a diverse world. You could use it to help the children to empathise with the feelings of those who are bullied.

Poems on an issue (page 64) develops an appreciation of how poets express feelings about the same issue, through exploring the imagery and language they use. It could be linked with work in citizenship and could be the basis for a class or group debate to encourage speaking and listening. Suitable poems include 'The Song of the Fir' (Eleanor Farjeon), 'The Prayer of the Tree' (Anon), 'For Forest' (Grace Nichols), 'To George Pulling Buds' (Adelaide O'Keeffe), 'Trees' (Harold Munro), 'Felled Trees' (Ruth Dallas), 'Throwing a Tree' (Thomas Hardy), 'Ten Tall Oak Trees' (Richard Edwards), 'The Axe in the Wood' (Clifford Dyment) and others from *Shades of Green* (Anne Harvey, Red Fox).

Using the CD-ROM

The PC CD-ROM included with this book contains an easy-to-use software program that allows you to print out pages from the book, to view them (e.g. on an interactive whiteboard) or to customise the activities to suit the needs of your pupils.

Getting started

It's easy to run the software. Simply insert the CD-ROM into your CD drive and the disk should autorun and launch the interface in your web browser.

If the disk does not autorun, open 'My Computer' and select the CD drive, then open the file 'start.html'.

Please note: this CD-ROM is designed for use on a PC. It will also run on most Apple Macintosh computers in Safari however, due to the differences between Mac and PC fonts, you may experience some unavoidable variations in the typography and page layouts of the activity sheets.

The Menu screen

Four options are available to you from the main menu screen.

The first option takes you to the Activity Sheets screen, where you can choose an activity sheet to edit or print out using Microsoft Word.

If you do not have the Microsoft Office suite, you might like to consider using OpenOffice instead. This is a multi-platform and multi-lingual office suite, and an 'open-source' project. It is compatible with all other major office suites, and the product is free to download, use and distribute. The homepage for OpenOffice on the Internet is: www.openoffice.org.)

The second option on the main menu screen opens a PDF file of the entire book using Adobe Reader (see below). This format is ideal for printing out copies of the activity sheets or for displaying them, for example on an interactive whiteboard.

The third option allows you to choose a page to edit from a text-only list of the activity sheets, as an alternative to the graphical interface on the Activity Sheets screen.

Adobe Reader is free to download and to use. If it is not already installed on your computer, the fourth link takes you to the download page on the Adobe website.

You can also navigate directly to any of the three screens at any time by using the tabs at the top.

The Activity Sheets screen

This screen shows thumbnails of all the activity sheets in the book. Rolling the mouse over a thumbnail highlights the page number and also brings up a preview image of the page.

Click on the thumbnail to open a version of the page in Microsoft Word (or an equivalent software program, see above.) The full range of editing tools are available to you here to customise the page to suit the needs of your particular pupils. You can print out copies of the page or save a copy of your edited version onto your computer.

The Index screen

This is a text-only version of the Activity Sheets screen described above. Choose an activity sheet and click on the 'download' link to open a version of the page in Microsoft Word to edit or print out.

Technical support

If you have any questions regarding the *100% New Developing Literacy* or *Developing Mathematics* software, please email us at the address below. We will get back to you as quickly as possible.

educationalsales@acblack.com

Adventure story structure

- **Write the main events of an adventure story in the flow-chart.**

Title _____

Author _____

Opening

[box]

> Does the author describe the setting and introduce the character...

> ... or introduce a problem right away?

The trigger

[box]

> What starts the action? A character, an event?

> Does the main character change?

The adventure: places and events

[boxes connected by arrows]

Ending

[box]

> Does the character return home or go elsewhere? Has he or she changed, or learned anything?

Teachers' note Use this with any adventure story. Ask the children whether the action begins right away or there is a long introduction describing the setting and introducing the characters. Ask them what triggers the adventure: an event, news, a discovery, a character. They can then summarise the main events and make a note of their settings and write a brief note on the ending.

**100% New Developing Literacy
Understanding and Responding
to Texts: Ages 10–11**
© A & C BLACK

The language of adventure

- **Underline the words and phrases that add excitement to the adventure:**
  - **green: verbs or verb phrases**
  - **blue: adjectives or adjective phrases**
  - **red: nouns or noun phrases.**

For a moment Peter did not understand. Then, when he saw all the other creatures start forward and heard Aslan say with a wave of his paw, 'Back! Let the Prince win his spurs,' he did understand, and set off running as hard as he could to the pavilion. And there he saw a dreadful sight.

The Naiads and Dryads were scattering in every direction. Lucy was running towards him as fast as her short legs would carry her and her face was as white as paper. Then he saw Susan make a dash for a tree, and swing herself up, followed by a huge grey beast. At first Peter thought it was a bear. Then he saw that it looked like an Alsatian, though it was far too big to be a dog. Then he realised that it was a wolf – a wolf standing on its hind legs, with its front paws against the tree-trunk, snapping and snarling. All the hair on its back stood up on end. Susan had not been able to get higher than the second big branch. One of her legs hung down so that her foot was only an inch or two above the snapping teeth. Peter wondered why she did not get higher or at least take a better grip; then he realized that she was just going to faint and that if she fainted she would fall off.

Peter did not feel very brave; indeed, he felt he was going to be sick. But that made no difference to what he had to do. He rushed straight up to the monster and aimed a slash of his sword at its side. That stroke never reached the Wolf. Quick as lightning it turned round, its eyes flaming, and its mouth wide open in a howl of anger. If it had not been so angry that it simply had to howl it would have got him by the throat at once. As it was – though all this happened too quickly for Peter to think at all – he had just time to duck down and plunge his sword, as hard as he could, between the brute's forelegs into its heart. Then came a horrible, confused moment like something in a nightmare. He was tugging and pulling and the Wolf seemed neither alive nor dead, and its bared teeth knocked against his forehead, and everything was blood and heat and hair. A moment later he found that the monster lay dead and he had drawn his sword out of it and was straightening his back and rubbing the sweat off his face and out of his eyes. He felt tired all over.

From *The Lion, the Witch and the Wardrobe* by C. S. Lewis

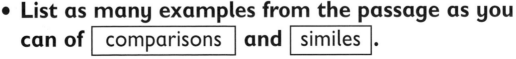

NOW TRY THIS!

- **List as many examples from the passage as you can of** comparisons **and** similes **.**
- **Describe the effect of each example.**

Teachers' note Use this to show how powerful language is used to create an atmosphere. How did the children feel when reading it? Discuss the atmosphere and pace of the passage, how these change and how the author creates these effects. The children could write notes on a 'hill' diagram to show how the tension builds up to a climax and is then released.

100% New Developing Literacy Understanding and Responding to Texts: Ages 10–11 © A & C BLACK

Mystery

- Circle in red the ☐flashbacks☐ that say what happened in the past.
- Underline in green the sentence that introduces the ☐mystery☐.
- Tell a friend any questions the passage makes you ask.
- Write them on the back of this page.

When, suddenly, on an ordinary Wednesday, it seemed to Barney that the world tilted and ran down-hill in all directions, he knew he was about to be haunted again. It had happened when he was younger but he had thought that being haunted was a babyish thing that you grew out of, like crying when you fell over, or not having a bike.

'Remember Barney's imaginary friends, Mantis, Bigbuzz and Ghost?' Claire – his stepmother – sometimes said. 'The garden seems empty now that they've gone. I quite miss them.'

But she was really pleased perhaps because, being so very real to Barney, they had become too real for her to laugh over. Barney had been sorry to lose them, but he wanted Claire to feel comfortable living with him. He could not remember his own mother and Claire had come as a wonderful surprise, giving him a hug when he came home from school, asking him about his day, telling him about hers, arranging picnics and unexpected parties and helping him with hard homework. It seemed worth losing Mantis, Bigbuzz and Ghost and the other kind phantoms that had been his friends for so many days before Claire came.

Yet here it was beginning again… the faint dizzy twist in the world around him, the thin singing drone as if some tiny insect were trapped in the curling mazes of his ear. Barney looked up at the sky searching for a ghost but there was only a great blueness like a weight pressing down on him. He looked away quickly, half expecting to be crushed into a sort of rolled-out gingerbread boy in an enormous stretched-out school uniform. Then he saw his ghost on the footpath beside him.

A figure was slowly forming out of the air: a child – quite a little one, only about four or five – struggling to be real. A curious pale face grew clearer against a halo of shining hair, silver gold hair that curled and crinkled, fading into the air like bright smoke. The child was smiling. It seemed to be having some difficulty in seeing Barney so that he felt that he might be the one who was not quite real. Well, he was used to feeling that. In the days before Claire he had often felt that he himself couldn't be properly heard or seen. But then Mantis had taken time to become solid and Ghost had always been dim and smoky. So Barney was not too surprised to see the ghost looking like a flat paper doll stuck against the air by some magician's glue. Then it became round and real, looking alive, but old-fashioned and strange, in its blue velvet suit and lace collar. A soft husky voice came out of it.

'Barnaby's dead!' it said.

From The Haunting by Margaret Mahy

NOW TRY THIS!

- Cover the passage.
- Describe how the ghost appears.
- List some words from the passage to support your answer.

> Does he appear suddenly, smoothly, calmly, with a great effort?

Teachers' note Use this to introduce *The Haunting* or to develop the children's awareness of the structure of different mystery stories. Explain that this is the opening of the story and ask whether there is a slow build-up or the action begins right away. Ask why 'mystery' is a good description of the genre: focus on the questions it raises and discuss how these make readers want to read on.

100% New Developing Literacy
Understanding and Responding
to Texts: Ages 10–11
© A & C BLACK

A tale with tension: 1

Read this passage. Notice the build-up of tension **.**

1 At first it was just a tickle, which Twig swatted away in his sleep. He smacked his lips drowsily and rolled over onto his side. Nestling in his cot of leaves beneath the ancient spreading tree, Twig looked so young and small and vulnerable.

2 A long, thin squirmy creature was doing the tickling. As Twig's breathing grew more regular once again, it wriggled around in mid-air directly in front of his face. It flexed and writhed in the warm air each time Twig breathed out. All at once, it darted forwards and began probing the skin around the boy's mouth.

3 Twig grumbled sleepily, and his hand brushed at his lips. The squirmy creature dodged the slender fingers, and scurried up into the dark tunnel of warmth above.

4 Twig sat bolt upright, instantly wide awake. His heart pounded. There was something up his left nostril!

5 He grabbed his nose and squeezed it till his eyes watered. Abruptly, the whatever-it-was scraped down over the soft membrane inside his nose, and was out. Twig winced, and his eyes screwed shut with pain. His heart pounded all the more furiously. What was there? What could it possibly be? Fear and hunger wrestled with one another in the pit of Twig's stomach.

6 Scarcely daring to look, Twig peered out through the crack in one eye. Catching sight of a flash of emerald-green, Twig feared the worst, and scuttled back on his hands and feet. The next moment, he slipped, his legs shot out in front of him and he came crashing down on his elbows. He stared back into the gloomy half-light of the new morning. The wriggly green creature had not moved.

7 'I'm being silly,' Twig muttered. 'It's just a caterpillar.'

8 Leaning back, he squinted up into the dark canopy. Behind black leaves, the sky had turned from brown to red. The air was warm, but the backs of his legs were damp with the early morning moisture of the Deepwoods. It was time to make a move.

9 Twig climbed to his feet and was brushing the twigs and leaves out of the hammelhornskin waistcoat when – WHOOOOSH – the air hissed with a sound like a lashing whip. Twig gasped, and stared in frozen horror as the emerald green caterpillar lunged at him and flew round his outstretched wrist once, twice, three times.

0 'Aaaargh!' he screamed as sharp thorns dug into his skin – and he cursed himself for letting his guard slip.

1 For the wriggly green creature wasn't a caterpillar at all. It was a creeper; a tendril, the emerald tip of a long and viciously barbed vine that writhed and swayed through the shadowy forest like a serpent, seeking out warm-blooded prey. Twig had been lassoed by the terrible tarry vine.

From The Edge Chronicles: Beyond the Deepwoods by Paul Stewart and Chris Riddell

Teachers' note Notice the children's responses as they read the passage. Ask them which parts make them respond in this way. They could underline the powerful words and phrases. Ask how the connectives and the sentence structure help. Also point out the contrasts: Twig sleeping peacefully; feeling something squirming up his nose; grumbling sleepily; then sitting bolt upright.

100% New Developing Literacy
Understanding and Responding
to Texts: Ages 10–11
© A & C BLACK

A tale with tension: 2

- **Complete the key for the** `tension` **graph.**
- **Then complete the tension graph for the passage from *The Edge Chronicles*.**

 Think about how different levels of tension in a story make you feel and how you respond.

Key		
Level	Description	How I feel and respond
0	No tension	
1	Low tension	
2	Medium tension	
3	High tension	
4	Very high tension	
5	Unbearably high tension	

Tension graph

 Draw a line graph.

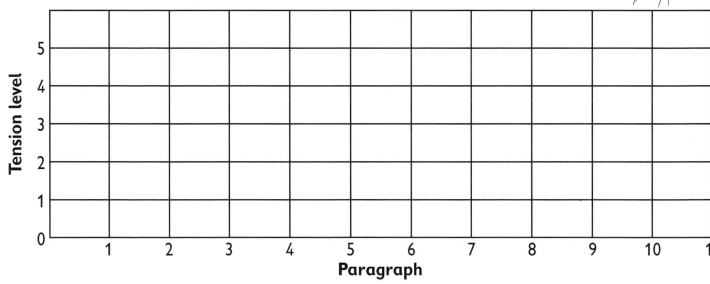

NOW TRY THIS!

- **Make a graph to show a different aspect of a story:**

| level of difficulty faced by a character | **or** | level of a character's happiness |

Teachers' note The children should first have read the passage on page 17 and described their feelings as they read it. Ask them to trace the build-up of disgust, horror and tension through each paragraph. You could reproduce the graph on the interactive whiteboard. Ask the children first to identify the climax – where the tension is at its worst – and mark this paragraph as 5 on the graph.

100% New Developing Literacy
Understanding and Responding
to Texts: Ages 10–11
© A & C BLACK

Parody

● **Read this poem.**

The Owl and the Astronaut

The owl and the astronaut
Sailed through space
In their intergalactic ship
They kept hunger at bay
With three pills a day
And drank through a protein drip.

The owl dreamed of mince
And slices of quince
And remarked how life had gone flat;
'It may be all right
To fly faster than light
But I preferred the boat and the cat.'

Gareth Owen

● **Of which famous poem is this a** [parody] **?**
● **Read the original poem.**
● **In which ways is this poem similar to the original?**
● **Give examples.**

> Think about characters, words, rhyme pattern, rhythm, storyline and so on.

Similarity	Examples	
	Original poem	**Parody**

NOW TRY THIS!

● **Write your ideas for another parody of the same poem.**

eachers' note The children should first have read, and have access to a copy of, 'The Owl and the ssycat' by Edward Lear (see *Notes on the activities*, page 7). They will notice that this parodies nly the first verse of the poem. As a further extension they could continue the parody to the next r subsequent verses.

**100% New Developing Literacy
Understanding and Responding
to Texts: Ages 10–11**
© A & C BLACK

The quest

- Draw and write the details of a | quest | story you have read.

Title _____ Author _____

Main character

Setting

Problems and challenges

1

2

3

4

5

6

The quest

NOW TRY
THIS!

- Write a | summary | of the story.

Teachers' note Use this to help the children to analyse the structure of a story that involves a quest (possibly an adventure story, a traditional tale, myth or legend). After reading the opening chapter ask them to make notes about the character and setting and to identify the quest. As they read on, they can identify any tasks the character has to complete in order to achieve the objective.

100% New Developing Literacy
Understanding and Responding
to Texts: Ages 10–11
© A & C BLACK

Quest choice

- How do a character's choices affect the outcome of the story?
- Complete the flow-chart.

Title _____

Author _____

Character _____

Situation

Choices

Outcomes

Write notes.

NOW TRY THIS!

- How do these choices affect other situations in the story?

Teachers' note Use this with any quest-type adventure story. Pause wherever a character has a choice and ask the children what might happen as a result of each choice. Discuss how what eventually happened matched their prediction and what might have happened had the character chosen differently. You could record all the choices and their outcomes on a large flow-chart.

100% New Developing Literacy
Understanding and Responding to Texts: Ages 10–11
© A & C BLACK

World to world

- **How do story characters move from one 'world' to a different one?**
- **Record what happens in stories you read.**

Examples

Tom's Midnight Garden	The Lion, the Witch and the Wardrobe	Harry Potter and the Deathly Hallows	Alice's Adventures in Wonderland
Philippa Pearce	C.S. Lewis	J.K. Rowling	Lewis Carroll

Story and author	The different worlds and how characters move between them

NOW TRY THIS!

- **Make notes about different 'worlds' for a story you will write.**

Teachers' note Discuss any stories the children have read in which characters move from one 'world' to another. Ask them how the different worlds are related and how and where the character can move between them. They could also make notes about any changes to the character when he or she is in the other world and to what extent he or she changes back when returning to their original world.

100% New Developing Literacy
Understanding and Responding
to Texts: Ages 10–11
© A & C BLACK

Adventure cards: 1

Characters

a boy

a girl

a mermaid

a young troll

an elf

a clockwork doll

Settings

a Tudor town

a forest

a modern house

an island

underground

a moor

Teachers' note Use this with page 24. Copy each set onto different coloured card to make it easy to distinguish characters, settings, quests and challenges or write the category name on the back of each card before they are cut out. Continued on page 24.

**100% New Developing Literacy
Understanding and Responding
to Texts: Ages 10–11
© A & C BLACK**

Adventure cards: 2

Quests

to find a lost parent, brother or sister

to collect an important document

to stop something evil happening

to identify a troublemaker

to find an important object

to find a secret place

Challenges

monsters

swamps

fire

water

spells

illness and plagues

Teachers' note Continued from page 23. The children select 'ingredients' for an adventure story, based on what they have learned from stories they have read. They could begin with any set and choose other ingredients to match.

**100% New Developing Literacy
Understanding and Responding
to Texts: Ages 10–11**
© A & C BLACK

Reading Skellig: 1

• ## Read this passage.

I found him in the garage on a Sunday afternoon. It was the day after we moved into Falconer Road. The winter was ending. Mum had said we'd be moving just in time for the spring. Nobody else was there. Just me. The others were inside the house with Doctor Death, worrying about the baby.

He was lying there in the darkness behind the tea chests, in the dust and dirt. It was as if he'd been there forever. He was filthy and pale and dried out and I thought he was dead. I couldn't have been more wrong. I'd soon begin to see the truth about him, that there'd never been another creature like him in the world.

We called it the garage because that's what the estate agent, Mr Stone, called it. It was more like a demolition site or a rubbish dump or like one of those ancient warehouses they keep pulling down at the quay. Stone led us down the garden, tugged the door open and shone his little torch into the gloom. We shoved our heads in at the doorway with him.

'You have to see it with your mind's eye,' he said. 'See it cleaned, with new doors and the roof repaired. See it as a wonderful two-car garage.'

He looked at me with a stupid grin on his face. 'Or something for you, lad – a hideaway for you and your mates. What about that, eh?'

I looked away. I didn't want anything to do with him. All the way round the house it had been the same. Just see it in your mind's eye. Just imagine what could be done. All the way round I kept thinking of the old man, Ernie Myers, that had lived here on his own for years. He'd been dead nearly a week before they found him under the table in the kitchen.

That's what I saw when Stone told us about seeing with the mind's eye. He even said it when we got to the dining room and there was an old cracked toilet sitting there in the corner behind a plywood screen. I just wanted him to shut up, but he whispered that towards the end Ernie couldn't manage the stairs. His bed was brought in here and a toilet was put in so everything was easy for him. Stone looked at me like he didn't think I should know about such things. I wanted to get out to get back to our old house again, but Mum and Dad took it all in. They went on like it was going to be some big adventure. They bought the house. They started cleaning it and scrubbing it and painting it. Then the baby came too early. And here we were.

Chapter 1 of *Skellig* by David Almond

Teachers' note Use this with page 26. Give the children time to read and respond to the passage, then ask them if it makes them want to read the rest of the book. Discuss why this is: probably because they want to know who 'he' is, what he is going to do and how this will affect the boy in the story.

100% New Developing Literacy
Understanding and Responding
to Texts: Ages 10–11
© A & C BLACK

Reading Skellig: 2

- **Complete the** reading journal **for Chapter 1 of** *Skellig*.
- **Write notes.**

How the book is written

Tense _____   Person _____

What I know about the main character

> Boy or girl? Name? Age? Family?

What I know about the main character's life

How the main character feels

> Give evidence.

How the author makes the reader want to read on

Teachers' note Use this with page 25. After the children have completed the reading journal ask them what they know about the main character and how: for example, the word *lad*, used by the estate agent, tells the reader that he is a boy; the words *I looked away* show the boy's dislike of the estate agent and help to express his feelings against the family's move to a new house.

100% New Developing Literacy Understanding and Responding to Texts: Ages 10–11 © A & C BLACK

Character conflicts in Skellig

- Draw lines to link the characters who have ⬚conflicts⬚ in *Skellig*.
- On the lines write notes about the conflicts.

Mina

Skellig

Coot

Michael's father

Michael

Leakey

Michael's mother

Mrs Dando

Dr 'Death'

NOW TRY THIS!

- Make a flow-chart to trace the relationship between Michael and Mina.
- Write notes and give evidence.

Teachers' note This page supports further reading of the book. Copy it onto A3 paper. The children might find there are several lines of conflict which change during the story: for example, Michael is fascinated by Skellig but disgusted by some of his traits: the flies he eats, his foul breath and so on. Coot and Leakey are initially disdainful towards Mina but develop respect for her.

100% New Developing Literacy
Understanding and Responding
to Texts: Ages 10–11
© A & C BLACK

Themes in Skellig

- **Look for mentions of the baby, the new house, birds and angels in *Skellig*.**

The baby

The new house

Birds

Angels

NOW TRY THIS!

- **How are all the** themes **connected?**
- **Make notes and give examples from the text.**

28

Teachers' note The children could use sticky notes to mark mentions of the four examples. Why has the author focused on them? How are they linked? (For example, owls, wings and angels.) Explain that these links build into themes: the baby forms part of the theme of illness and medicine (the baby is ill; at the hospital Michael asks a doctor about arthritis so that he can help Skellig).

100% New Developing Literacy Understanding and Responding to Texts: Ages 10–11 © A & C BLACK

The Piano: themes

- **Which six** themes **are in** *The Piano*? ✔
- **Give evidence on the chart.**

friendship		hatred		childhood	

love		marriage		death	

slavery		war		money	

Write notes.

Theme	Evidence

Teachers' note Remind the children of previous work on this film: ask what it is about. What are the main events of the pianist's life? The children should watch the film again and note what it says about his life. Ask them in what ways it is similar to the lives of many other men of his age: they fell in love, married, had children and grandchildren, were called up for National Service and fought in wars.

100% New Developing Literacy
Understanding and Responding
to Texts: Ages 10–11
© A & C BLACK

- Listen to the music as you watch *The Piano*.
- Draw a line graph to show the [pace] of the music in different [scenes].

Pace

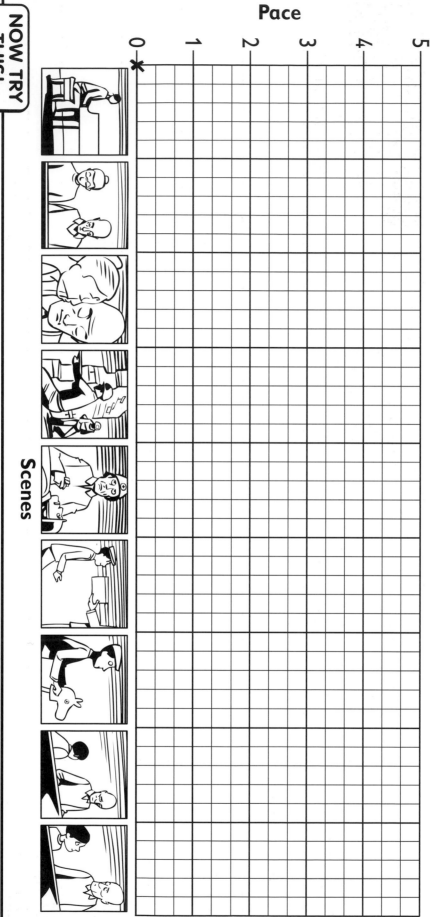

Scenes

Key
0 — music stops
1 — slowest
5 — quickest

- Explain how the music matches the mood of each scene.

Teachers' note Let the children watch the film *The Piano* again; this time focus on the music. Ask them to notice how it changes in speed, and even stops, at different points in the film. Encourage them to talk about how this matches the scenes and how it creates the mood for each scene.

100% New Developing Literacy
Understanding and Responding
to Texts: Ages 10–11
© A & C BLACK

The Piano: time links

- **How does the film-maker show changes from present → past → present?**
- **Write notes on the chart.**

Technique	The pianist's wife	Flashbacks	
		The war	His childhood
Gestures and movements			
Camera pan			
Editing of images			
Costume			

Think about the techniques.

NOW TRY THIS!

- **Who is the boy you see at the end of the film?**
- **Is this the past or the present?**
- **Explain your answers.**

Teachers' note This is based on the film *The Piano*. Ask the children what they remember about the angle from which some parts are filmed: low, eye-level, high, from the side, close-up, distant. Ask them to note when there is a flashback or return to the present and to identify the signal for this: a change of camera pan, a gesture, expression or movement or a costume change.

100% New Developing Literacy
Understanding and Responding
to Texts: Ages 10–11
© A & C BLACK

The Piano: memories

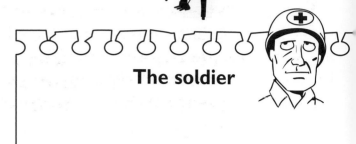

- **What memories might the other characters have of time spent with the pianist?**
- **Write notes on the notepads.**

The wife

The soldier

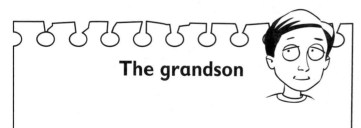

The grandson

NOW TRY THIS!

- **Write a paragraph about each character's memories.**
- **Think of a way of linking the paragraphs to tell a story.**

Teachers' note Ask the children about the other characters in the film: the pianist's wife, his soldier comrade, his grandson. What memories might they have of the pianist? The children could use evidence from the film to deduce some memories they might have in addition to those which can be inferred from what is actually seen.

100% New Developing Literacy
Understanding and Responding
to Texts: Ages 10–11
© A & C BLACK

● **Read the passage.**

John Lennon (1940–1980)

John Winston Lennon was born on 9th October 1940 at Liverpool Maternity Hospital. By 1946 his parents, Alfred and Julia Lennon, had split up. John lived with his mother and her new partner John ('Bobby') Dykins. Before long he went to live with Julia's sister Mimi Smith and her husband, George, who had no children, at their house, 'Mendips' in Menlove Avenue in Woolton, a suburb of Liverpool.

John attended Dovedale Primary School then, from September 1952, Quarry Bank High School. He went on to Liverpool College of Art.

Eventually John's mother bought a guitar for him. He used to sit on his bed singing and making up tunes until Mimi said that he had to go into the porch to play his guitar. She is said to have told him, 'The guitar is all very well as a hobby, but you'll never make a *living* out of it.'

In July 1958 Julia Lennon was run over by a car and killed in Menlove Avenue, on her way home from a visit to Mimi.

John and some friends at Quarry Bank formed a band – the Quarry Men. They used to play at local dances; then on 6th July 1957 they played at Woolton Parish Church garden fête. That was when John first met Paul McCartney. Some members of the group left and new ones joined them and in 1960 they became known as the Beatles.

They spent two years playing in clubs in Hamburg, Germany, and by 1962 the Beatles were George Harrison, John Lennon, Paul McCartney and Ringo Starr. That year John married Cynthia Powell.

When the Beatles came back from Hamburg they became regular players at the Cavern Club in Liverpool. A local record shop owner, Brian Epstein, became their manager and, in 1962, he secured a contract for them with the recording company Parlophone. That year they recorded their first single *Love Me Do*. Their second, *Please Please Me*, reached No. 1 in the charts in January 1963. John and Cynthia's son Julian was born a few months later – in April.

The Beatles' tour of the USA in 1964 made them world-famous. They were each awarded the MBE (Member of the British Empire) at Buckingham Palace in 1966. (John later sent his MBE back in protest against Britain's involvement in wars in Vietnam and Biafra.)

In 1968 John and Cynthia were divorced and in March 1969 he married Yoko Ono. By this time the members of the Beatles had developed their own, separate, careers and formally split up as a group in 1971.

That year John and Yoko went to live in New York.

On 8th December 1980 John was shot outside the apartment block in New York where he and Yoko lived.

eachers' note The children could read this in pairs or individually. Ask them if this biography resents unbiased facts or expresses an opinion, and how they can tell. Ask them what facts they ave learned from it. They could list these and verify them in other sources (see *Notes on the ctivities*, page 9) before they begin the questions on page 34.

100% New Developing Literacy Understanding and Responding to Texts: Ages 10–11 © A & C BLACK

33

Brief biography: 2

- **Read the brief** biography **of John Lennon.**
- **Write three questions it leaves unanswered.**
- **Find the answers from other** sources .

Questions   **Answers**

_____
_____
_____
_____
_____

Source _____

_____
_____
_____
_____

Source _____

_____
_____
_____
_____

Source _____

NOW TRY THIS!

- **Use your notes to help you to rewrite a paragraph from the brief biography.**
- **Add details.**

Teachers' note Use this with page 33. The children could discuss the facts they have learned from the biography and then make a note of anything it does not tell them: for example, why John Lennon lived with his aunt; what happened to his father; what qualifications he gained (if any) at school and college; who the original members of his group were; who shot him and why.

100% New Developing Literacy
Understanding and Responding
to Texts: Ages 10–11
© A & C BLACK

Different versions

- **Compare these** biographies **.**
- **Underline phrases that show** bias **.**
- **On a separate sheet list the** facts **and** opinions **.**

1 The Horrible Story of Henry the Eighth and his Wives

Henry's married life was more disgraceful than that of any other English king. He had six wives. First was Catherine of Aragon, mother of Queen Mary, whom he tired of and got rid of by divorce. She lived for some years afterwards, a saddened woman. Then came Anne Boleyn, his second wife, and mother of Queen Elizabeth, but Henry grew tired of her, fixed up a trial to show her guilty of treason and had her beheaded. Jane Seymour, his third wife, mother of Edward VI, died a natural death but Henry was soon ready to marry again. Anne of Cleves, the fourth, was soon divorced because Henry – who had not seen her before he married her – found her too plain for his liking. Catherine Howard, the fifth, he got rid of in the same way as Anne Boleyn. Last of all came Catherine Parr, his sixth wife, who was fortunate enough to outlive this callous man.

2 Henry VIII – the Unlucky Husband

Before Henry VIII became king, his father persuaded him to marry Catherine of Aragon, his brother's widow. As an obedient son, Henry did so, but he later realised that the marriage was illegal in the eyes of the Church because his wife had been his sister-in-law. Once he became king it was important for Henry to have an heir, preferably a son, to ensure the succession of his family as monarchs. Catherine had only one child who survived – a daughter. In order to have a son, Henry divorced her and married Anne Boleyn, but he was unlucky once again: she gave birth only to a daughter. She was unfaithful to him. By law, this was treason, for which the punishment was death, so she was beheaded. The unlucky king tried for a third time, but this wife, Jane Seymour, died twelve days after their son Edward was born. Edward was a sickly child and it was feared that he would not live to adulthood. Henry needed another son. His advisers chose his fourth wife for him, but they chose badly and Henry very soon divorced Anne of Cleves. Catherine Howard, his fifth wife, was no better than Anne Boleyn, so she too was beheaded. Then Henry married Catherine Parr, a good woman and devoted wife, but she did not give him another son.

NOW TRY THIS!

- **Find out more about the facts.**
- **Write a more balanced version of this section of Henry VIII's biography.**

Teachers' note Ask the children if these biographies present unbiased facts or express opinions, and how they can tell. They can then list the facts they find out from each one and check whether they agree before they identify and compare the opinions expressed by words such as *horrible*, *disgraceful*, *unlucky*, *saddened*, *callous*, *obedient*, *badly*, *no better than*.

100% New Developing Literacy Understanding and Responding to Texts: Ages 10–11 © A & C BLACK

• Read the passage.

I wish I could remember my coronation, the day I was crowned overall winner of the Litherland Baby Show at the age of eighteen months. I wish I could remember that morning in the backyard when I stood up in my pram to dip my dummy into a cloud and fell out, landing on my head, or that time I was kidnapped and held to ransom by Hungarian gypsies… All right, I was kidding about the kidnap, but I clearly remember being woken up in the middle of the night, and my sister and me being put into dressing gowns, the ones with silken rabbits stitched on, carried downstairs and hurried off to the air-raid shelter at the bottom of the road.

*The cord of my new dressing-gown
he helps me tie*

*Then on to my father's shoulder
held high*

*The world at night with my little eye
I spy*

*The moon close enough to touch
I try*

*Silver-painted elephants have learned
to fly*

*Giants fence with searchlights
in the sky*

*Too soon into the magic shelter
he and I*

*Air raids are so much fun
I wonder why*

*In the bunk below, a big boy
starts to cry.*

Although the fear of those adults around me may have been contagious, the only feelings I can remember were of excitement. The bunk beds in the shelter would have been crammed with children, the young ones laughing or crying, the older ones reading stories to them or singing, and the grown-ups coming and going, trying to make light of the situation. My father would have been a volunteer fireman, perhaps on duty outside, where the sky would have been fizzing with light and noise.

From *Said and Done* (Roger McGough's autobiography)

Teachers' note Ask the children how this is different from a biography: who wrote it, the structure, language (direct style) and person. Note the difference in sources between a biography and an autobiography (people writing about themselves can use their own memories as well as asking other people what they remember; they can also 'muse' about these memories and 'talk to' the reader).

**100% New Developing Literacy
Understanding and Responding
to Texts: Ages 10–11**
© A & C BLACK

Poetic autobiography: 2

- **Which parts of the** [autobiography] **come from**
  - **Roger McGough's memories**
  - **other people's memories**
  - **facts Roger McGough learned later?**
- **Write notes in the shapes.**

I remember

We remember

I learned later

NOW TRY THIS!

- **What pictures does the passage make you see in your mind?**
- **What sounds does it make you hear?**
- **Describe how the writer does this.**

eachers' note Use this with page 36. The children could first underline the events the writer imself remembers and then, in a different colour, those remembered by other people. Draw ttention to the way in which Roger McGough discusses his memories with the reader and omments on how he checked them with others.

100% New Developing Literacy
Understanding and Responding
to Texts: Ages 10–11
© A & C BLACK

Is this your life?

- **Use this page to organise your research about a person's life.**

Name of person _____

Why I chose this person _____

What I know about him or her	Evidence/Source
Facts	
Talents, interests, personal qualities	
His/her opinions	

My questions

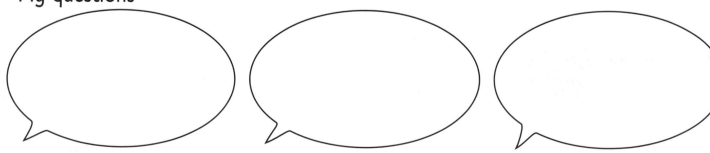

NOW TRY THIS!

- **Collect information to help you to answer your questions.**

Teachers' note This could be used to help the children to research the life of someone they have studied in history, science or another area of the curriculum. They could use a range of sources: the Internet, books, newspapers, magazines, CD-ROMs and, for a local person of note, the local library or museum archives and, where relevant, people who knew him or her.

100% New Developing Literacy
Understanding and Responding
to Texts: Ages 10–11
© A & C BLACK

In the newspaper: 1

① CAR VANDAL JAILED

Residents of Carrville breathed a sigh of relief when Luke Goode, 22, was jailed for the theft of more than five thousand car badges. Goode, of Station Road, never went out without a set of screwdrivers to unscrew or lever off the badges. Harry Leaf, 63, said he had replaced the badge on the front of his Porsche five times: 'As soon as I replaced the stolen badge the new one would go, too,' he said. 'I must have spent hundreds of pounds on badges and paintwork repairs.'

② COME TO GAOL

The Old Gaol houses a superb exhibition of instruments of punishment, original documents and life-sized models of cells. Curator Jean Warden said, 'I am delighted that the exhibition is ready. We have worked very hard on it.'

④ Clements

Paul and Julie Clements announce the birth of their son Nathan Philip, born on 4 November at Liverpool Maternity Hospital.

③ AERIALS

Supplied

Fitted

Repaired

Free estimates

All work fully guaranteed

Rufus Hyre

01234 567890

⑤ Pet or Pest?

Your opinion will depend on your lifestyle and priorities. Most people agree that rats and mice – in the wrong places (i.e. a hotel, restaurant or your home) – are pests, but there are many who keep them as pets. To a gamekeeper your much-loved family cat is a pest if it attacks pheasants. If your dog worries sheep a farmer treats it as a pest and is legally entitled to shoot it.

⑥ Scorpio

A lot can change between now and the full moon on the 9th. Aim high and you will not be disappointed.

⑦ HEALTHY LIFE PHOTOS

Send photographs of anything that sums up 'a healthy life' to the address at the top of the page. You can send prints or email digital photos (high resolution, please). They must have been taken between May and September this year.

Prizes include a year's free private health insurance, a year's supply of fresh fruit and vegetables, and a top-of-the-range digital camera.

Teachers' note Ask the children to consider the purpose of each article and for whom it was written. How can they tell? They could also consider why quotations are suitable in some but not in others. Page 40 helps them to analyse them in greater detail but some children might be able to identify the type of article without referring to the list of journalistic text types.

100% New Developing Literacy Understanding and Responding to Texts: Ages 10–11 © A & C BLACK

In the newspaper: 2

- Compare texts 1 to 7 on page 39.
- Decide what type of [newspaper text] they are.
- Complete the chart about their [purposes] and [features].

Journalistic texts include reports, competitions, horoscopes, announcements, advertisements, recounts, arguments.

Text	Type	Purpose	Tense	Person	Main sentence type	Other language features
1						
2						
3						
4						
5						
6						
7						

NOW TRY THIS!

- Collect other types of journalistic writing.
- Make a chart to record your observations about them.

Teachers' note Use this with page 39. You could also adapt it to help the children to analyse the style features of any journalistic writing. 'Other language features' could include verb voice (active/passive), connectives (simple/linking, time, cause/reason, purpose), how personal the language is and the level of formality.

100% New Developing Literacy Understanding and Responding to Texts: Ages 10–11 © A & C BLACK

The five Ws

- How well does the news │recount│ answer the five W questions?
- Write on the chart.
- Explain your evaluation.

Sour ending for sweet shop

A local sweet shop is to close after serving the community for more than a hundred years. Chouetts of Demerara Street was founded by the great-great-grandfather of Delia Sucrose, 34, who is heartbroken at the loss of the family's traditional business, which has hardly altered during the past century.

'We still use the old glass jars to store loose sweets, even though they are delivered in modern plastic ones,' she said. 'We use the original scales and weights and wrap the sweets in paper bags, as we have done for more than fifty years.'

Her husband, Lyle, is certain that new healthy eating trends have led to the shop's reduced sales: 'Youngsters these days don't run around as much as we used to. So they get fat if they eat sweets,' he said, adding that he didn't think a few sweets did any harm 'as long as you don't overdo it.'

Chouetts will serve its last customer on Friday 4 June. New owner Leticia O'Nions plans to turn the shop into a wholefoods café.

Question	Answer	☺	Explanation
Who?			
What?			
Where?			
When?			
Why?			

NOW TRY THIS!

- How could the recount give better answers?
- What other information would you have liked it to tell you?

Teachers' note Remind the children of earlier learning about journalistic writing: the importance of asking and answering the questions Who? What? Where? When? and Why? They should be able to answer these when reading news recounts. When evaluating how well it answers them, they should consider whether it makes them want to ask questions and what is left unanswered.

100% New Developing Literacy
Understanding and Responding
to Texts: Ages 10–11
© A & C BLACK

The same but different

- Compare different newspapers' versions of the same story.

What are the headlines?

Are the facts the same?

What is emphasised?

Is there any bias?

Subject of story _____

Newspaper	Headline	Facts	Emphasis – and how	Bias – and evidence

NOW TRY THIS!

- Which version do you think is the best, and why?

Give evidence from the text.

Teachers' note Enlarge this onto A3 paper. Provide several different newspaper reports of the same story. Ask the children to compare the facts given in each story (they could underline them). Discuss any discrepancies. How can they check which is correct? Ask them to identify words or phrases indicating opinions. Point out that opinions may be communicated through the connotations of words.

100% New Developing Literacy
Understanding and Responding
to Texts: Ages 10–11
© A & C BLACK

Radio news

- Listen to a radio news story.
- Write notes about how it was presented.

Introduction

The story

_____

_____

_____

_____

_____

_____

_____

Ending

_____

_____

_____

_____

_____

_____

_____

How was the story introduced? A newspaper uses a headline.

Did the same newsreader tell the story? What other people were involved? Where did this part of the broadcast come from?

What changed between the story and the summary? Think about people, location, sound.

NOW TRY THIS!

- Compare the radio news with a newspaper version of the same story.
- Describe the advantages and disadvantages, similarities and differences.

Teachers' note Record a suitable radio news item or let the children listen to a live news programme online. Ask them to notice how and by whom the news stories are introduced, where there are changes in voice and location, also how sound is used to communicate information and atmosphere. Ensure they understand terms like _presenter_, _studio_, _location_, _audio_.

**100% New Developing Literacy
Understanding and Responding
to Texts: Ages 10–11**
© A & C BLACK

Television news

- **Describe how a** television news **story is presented.**

Introduction

Visuals

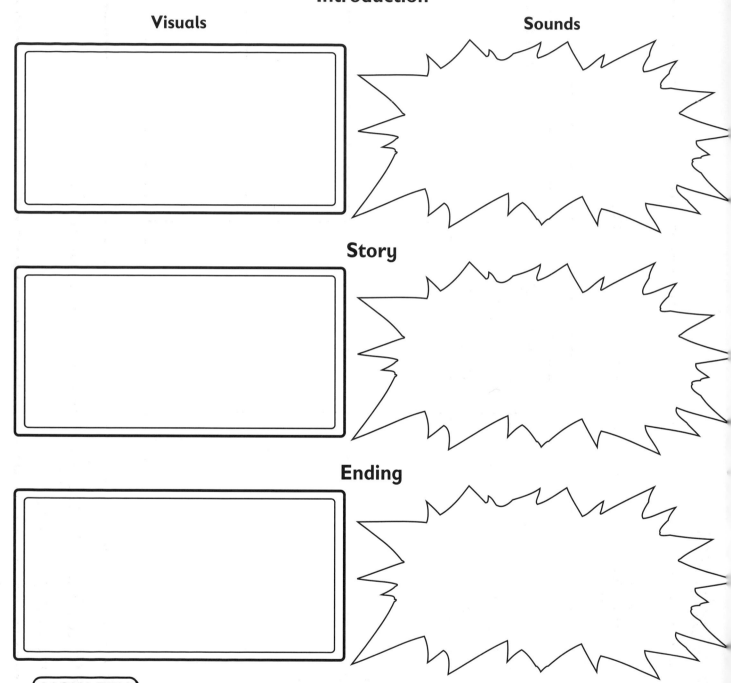

Sounds

Story

Ending

NOW TRY THIS!

- **Compare this television news story with the** radio **and** newspaper **versions.**
- **List any advantages and disadvantages of television.**

Teachers' note For this you could record a suitable television news item or let the children watch a live news programme. As they make notes they should think about the 'five Ws' and write only the main points.

100% New Developing Literacy Understanding and Responding to Texts: Ages 10–11 © A & C BLACK

Different stations

- **Compare the same** news story **on different radio stations.**

Subject of story _____

Radio station	Structure one newsreader/interview/ reporter on location?	Language formal/informal? complex/simple?	Evidence

NOW TRY THIS!

- **What kind of** audience **was each broadcast for?**
- **Explain your answer.**

Teachers' note This activity requires three radio programmes about the same news story: for example from Radio 4, Radio 1, a local radio station or a children's radio news programme. Remind the children of what is meant by complex, simple, formal and informal language: focus on person, use of colloquial language, length of sentences and vocabulary.

100% New Developing Literacy Understanding and Responding to Texts: Ages 10–11 © A & C BLACK

The whole programme

- **Compare two** television news **programmes.**

Programme _____ | Programme _____

Presenters

Write their names and the parts they present: news, business, money, sport, weather.

Studio arrangement

Do the presenters stand, sit on a sofa or behind a desk...?

Links

How does one item lead on to the next?

Graphics and locations

How are graphics and different locations used?

NOW TRY THIS!

- **Describe how the programmes keep viewers interested.**

Teachers' note For this the children could watch programmes from different television channels or from different times of the day. Remind them of terms such as *presenter, studio, location, graphics, audio*. Ask them to notice who and where the presenters are and whether they are standing, seated or moving around. Point out that parts of broadcast programmes are linked.

100% New Developing Literacy
Understanding and Responding
to Texts: Ages 10–11
© A & C BLACK

For, against or balanced

- **Cut out the cards.**
- **Sort the comments.**

| for | against | balanced |

Topic: Whether or not children under 12 should be allowed out after 7pm without an adult.

No responsible parents would let their children go out unaccompanied. If the children are harmed or get into trouble it's the parents' fault.

Alma Mater, 34, full-time home-maker

It depends on the children – their age, how capable they are at looking after themselves and where they are. They might be safe in rural areas miles from a town but not near a busy main road or in part of a town or city where there are many people they don't know.

Stan Dinfield, 61, farmer

Children can't develop a sense of responsibility if adults are always watching their every move. They can only develop good habits for personal safety through practice.

Rita Rome, 19, trainee counsellor

They shouldn't be allowed out at any time unsupervised. Anything could happen to them.

Mona Lott, 96, retired

It's difficult to let children out without an adult for the first time. You have to prepare them for it and begin with places that are close to home and at the safest times.

Dilip Singh, 59, politician

We're not stupid. Of course we should be allowed out after 7pm. Up to 10pm is fine if you're 10 to 12 years old but not if you're 3.

Stella Bright, 10, pupil

There are too many evil people about these days. You can't let children go far from home at any time.

Orla Roundace, 47, jobseeker

Children can be harmed at home, so they are just as safe outside the home.

Serena Tome, 18, student

NOW TRY THIS!

- **Add other points of your own: for and against to make a balanced argument.**

Teachers' note The children should cut out the comments and sort them into sets: 'for', 'against' or balanced'. To encourage speaking and listening ask them to work in groups: they could take turns o allocate a comment to a set but should justify their sorting and check whether the others agree.

100% New Developing Literacy
Understanding and Responding
to Texts: Ages 10–11
© A & C BLACK

Audience and purpose: 1

- **Read these two** arguments .

1 Be healthy – say no to TV

Television can damage your health. If you sit still for hours at a time, you use a lot less energy than if you are moving. But you don't eat less – in fact, you are likely to eat more if you watch TV. Most of us like to snack in front of the box. Not only do you eat more when you watch TV, but you also eat the WRONG foods: fatty and salty foods such as crisps, sugary sweets.

- You eat more and exercise less, so you get fatter.
- You eat unhealthy foods, so you are less healthy.
- You exercise less. This is bad for your heart and other muscles.

There are some good TV programmes – you should choose the one to watch carefully and then switch off afterwards.

2 Health threat from TV

Television is "the greatest unacknowledged health threat of our time" with 15 separate risks to couch potato children, a psychologist claimed.

Dr Aric Sigman is demanding daily viewing limits to help curb health problems ranging from obesity and short-sightedness to premature puberty. He believes youngsters under three should watch no television at all and parents should banish all TV sets from bedrooms.

In a report in a science journal, Dr Sigman lists 15 ways that exposure to TV screens can harm youngsters. These include raised risk of obesity and heart disease due to higher cholesterol and hormonal changes that disrupt sleep and even lower immunity. Among other potential hazards are short attention spans and learning problems.

Dr Sigman, an associate fellow of the British Psychological Society, told MPs yesterday that TV viewing should be rationed with a system of "recommended daily allowances", similar to guidelines for salt intake. Children aged three to seven should be limited to 30 minutes a day while seven to 12-year-olds should watch only an hour a day.

His report claims that too many hours spent slumped in front of screens hampers brain development since TV viewing, unlike reading, fails to provide growing brains with the stimulation needed to foster analytical thinking.

From the *Daily Mail* http://www.dailymail.co.uk/pages/live/articles/news/news.html?in_article_id=450162&in_page_id=177

Teachers' note The children should read and compare the two arguments about the topic of children's time spent watching television and identify their target audiences. Ask them to discuss these with a partner or group and to say how they can tell what type of audience they are for. They can then use page 49 to help them to organise their decisions and comments.

100% New Developing Literacy Understanding and Responding to Texts: Ages 10–11 © A & C BLACK

Audience and purpose: 2

- **Tell each audience which** `argument` **is addressed to them and why.**
- **Give evidence from the texts.**

Think about language: formal, informal, simple, difficult.

Children

Text ☐ is for you because

_____

_____

_____

_____

Parents

Text ☐ is for you because

_____

_____

_____

_____

NOW TRY THIS!

- **Rewrite Text 1 for a younger audience – aged 3 to 5.**

Change the type of language. Add pictures.

Teachers' note Use this with page 48 or with another pair of argument texts – one written for an audience of children and one for adults. Invite volunteers to read their comments to the class and encourage the others to notice any assumptions they make about the chosen audience.

100% New Developing Literacy Understanding and Responding to Texts: Ages 10–11
© A & C BLACK

Mobile phones – good or bad?

- **Read about mobile phones:**

| reports | recounts | arguments | persuasive texts |

- **Record the points** for **and** against **children having mobile phones**

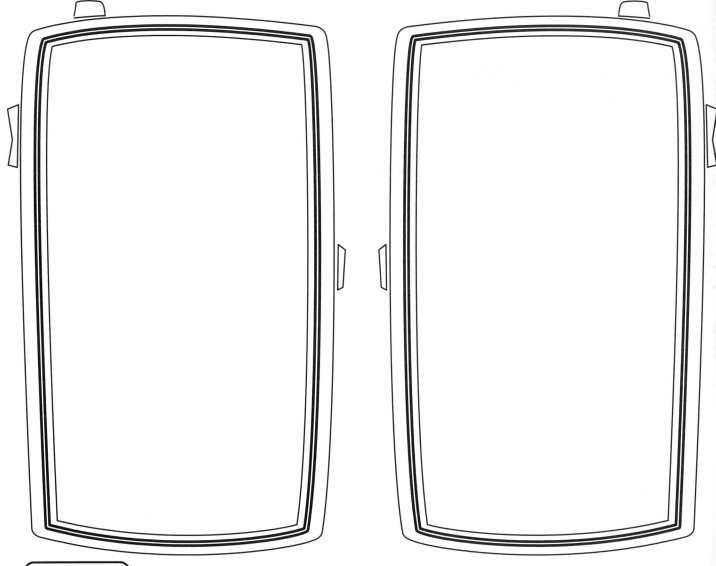

NOW TRY THIS!

- **Write a** summary **of the points you listed.**
- **Think about the importance of each point.**

Some points might be more important than others.

Teachers' note Ask the children to read or listen to reports about the use of mobile phones by children (see *Useful websites* on page 6) and to identify and make notes about points for and against. Ask them to read through the points they have made, bearing in mind their own views on the topic, and to decide whether their argument might be biased.

50

100% New Developing Literacy Understanding and Responding to Texts: Ages 10–11 © A & C BLACK

In agreement

- **Compare the two agreements.**
- **Are they** [formal] **or** [informal]? ✔
- **Underline the words and phrases that show this. Use red for formal language and green for informal language.**

①

You can borrow my bike if you lend me your scooter. I've checked with my mum and she says it's OK.

Great! Thanks. When?

On Saturday.

My dad says that's OK. But he said to ask you not to leave it outside shops or anywhere it can get nicked.

OK. I won't do that. Will you do the same with my bike?

Yes. Fair enough.

Formal		Informal	

② **16. Cycle Hire.**

a) All hired cycles remain the property of the Company and shall not be sold, hired or loaned out by the Client.

b) The Client acknowledges that the cycle hired is in good condition and undertakes to return the cycle and any accessories in that same condition, or to make a payment to the Company, immediately on demand, sufficient to return the cycle to that condition.

c) The Company shall not be liable for any damage or loss arising from the Client's use of the equipment. The Client shall indemnify the Company against any claim howsoever arising as a result of the Client's use of the cycle during the period of hire.

d) In the event that the cycle and/or any accessories are lost or stolen the Client shall indemnify the Company for the costs of replacing those items. Should the equipment subsequently be returned in a satisfactory condition these moneys will be repaid.

e) The Client will ensure that the cycle is adequately secured when not in use and will immediately notify the Company or one of its representatives in the event of any theft, loss, breakdown or other occurrence relating to the cycle or associated accessories.

f) All moneys due in relation to the hire of cycles will be added to the tour cost and will be payable in accordance with the Company's booking conditions.

From http://www.cycleactive.co.uk/terms.html

Formal		Informal	

eachers' note The children should decide whether each agreement is formal or informal and then
egin to identify the words and phrases that helped them to arrive at their decision: for example,
ocabulary, sentence length, bullet points, numbers, contracted words and colloquial words.

100% New Developing Literacy
**Understanding and Responding
to Texts: Ages 10–11**
© A & C BLACK

51

Informally

- **Write these words in** informal **language.**

Use a dictionary.   Use a thesaurus.

Formal	Informal
commence	
connected	
donate	
eject	
employment	
inform	
interim	
invoice	
malfunction	
procure	
prudent	
receive	
satisfactory	
select	
terminate	

NOW TRY THIS!

- **Write two versions of a short agreement between a pupil and a teacher on how to behave at school:** formal **and** informal **.**

Teachers' note The children could first work with a partner, explaining what they think each word means with their partner checking it in a dictionary and thesaurus, then they could write the most apt informal word for each of those in the list.

100% New Developing Literacy Understanding and Responding to Texts: Ages 10–11
© A & C BLACK

Site guides

- **Look at a** [leaflet] **and a** [website] **about a place.**
- **Notice the features they use.**
- **Comment on how well they use them.**

> Choose a local place of interest.

Place _____

Features	Comments	
	Leaflet	Website
Text: fonts		
colours		
sizes		
bullet points		
boxes		
Images: photographs		
drawings		
diagrams		
maps		
moving images		
Sounds: voice		
music		
other sounds		
Links to other sources		

NOW TRY THIS!

- **Evaluate how well the website used the Internet.**

> Could it have used other features? What else could it have done?

Teachers' note To prepare for this you could collect leaflets about local places of interest and bookmark their websites. Ask the children how much the leaflet and website they look at interest them, what attracts their attention and sparks their curiosity, and why: for example, the use of pictures, maps, cartoon characters, bullet points, animation, sound.

100% New Developing Literacy Understanding and Responding to Texts: Ages 10–11
© A & C BLACK

At the lead mines

- **Log on to the website of Killhope lead mine:**
  www.durham.gov.uk/killhope
- **What do you think you can find out here?**
- **Write your questions in the speech bubbles.**
- **See if the website helps to answer them.**

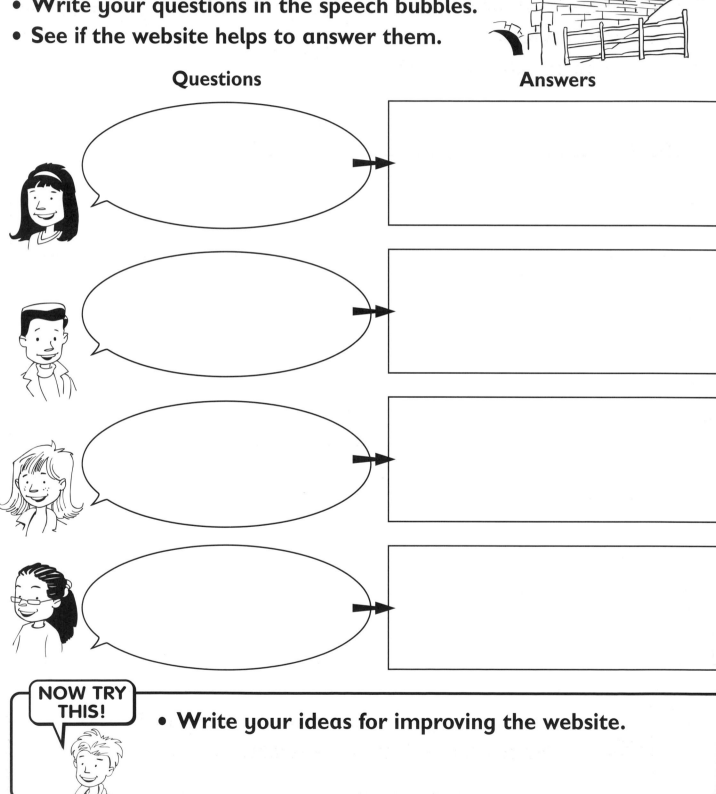

Questions	Answers

NOW TRY THIS!

- **Write your ideas for improving the website.**

Teachers' note Ask the children to scan the opening page of the website and to note the headings and links. Which of these do they want to click on, and why? Ask them what they think they can find out from each one. Discuss the information that potential visitors need: location, directions, parking, catering, when the lead mines operated and why they have become a visitor attraction.

100% New Developing Literacy
Understanding and Responding
to Texts: Ages 10–11
© A & C BLACK

Virtual tour

- **Look at a** ⎡virtual tour⎤ **of a place.**
- **What can visitors to the website find out?**
- **Complete the evaluation.**
- **Circle your answers.**
- **Write comments to explain them.**

Use the key.

Key

1 excellent	4 average
2 very good	5 poor
3 good	6 very poor

Photographs			Comments
Impact on the visitor	1 2 3	4 5 6	
How clearly they can be seen (use of zoom, focus and so on)	1 2 3	4 5 6	
How the visitor is helped to interpret photographs	1 2 3	4 5 6	
Information			
Type of information (whether all relevant information is given or anything is missing)	1 2 3	4 5 6	
Presentation of information (how easy it is to find and to follow)	1 2 3	4 5 6	

NOW TRY THIS!

- **How would you improve the virtual tour?**
- **Write an email to the website.**

Teachers' note Explain that an evaluation is meaningful if it is based on criteria rather than made according to likes and dislikes. The children could first discuss each of the criteria and agree what is meant by good or bad and then complete the page with a partner or group to encourage speaking and listening. During the plenary they could share their results and explore any big discrepancies.

100% New Developing Literacy Understanding and Responding to Texts: Ages 10–11
© A & C BLACK

- **What kind of 'personal' qualities does this poem give the city?**
- **Underline some in the list and add others.**
- **Underline the words in the poem that create these impressions.**
- **Link them to the qualities.**

City Jungle

Rain splinters town.

Lizard cars cruise by;
their radiators grin.

Thin headlights stare –
shop doorways keep
their mouths shut.

At the roadside
hunched houses cough.

Newspapers shuffle by,
hands in their pockets.
The gutter gargles.

A motorbike snarls;
Dustbins flinch.

Streetlights bare
their yellow teeth.
The motorway's
cat-black tongue
lashes across
the glistening back
of the tarmac night.

Pie Corbett

Personal qualities

calm
careless
careful
dangerous
evil
friendly
fussy
gentle
jolly
menacing
quiet
rough

_____

_____

_____

_____

_____

NOW TRY THIS!

- **Add a verb to [personify] each of these:**

postboxes _yawn_   spotlights _____   cars _____

streetlights _____   branches _____   roots _____

Teachers' note After reading the poem with the children ask them what the city is like. They should support their answers with examples from the poem. Ask them to choose an image and to talk about the picture it conjures up in their mind. Focus on the connotations of words: for example, why the poet chose the word *snarls* for the sound of the motorbike.

100% New Developing Literacy Understanding and Responding to Texts: Ages 10–11
© A & C BLACK

City Jungle: 2

- Plan a tableau of the city in 'City Jungle'
by Pie Corbett.

Work with
a group.

Cast (and descriptions)

_____   _____

_____   _____

_____   _____

Labelled plan of scene

Stage directions

Character	Action	Sound (if any)

NOW TRY THIS!

- Enact the scene with your group.
- Compare this with the poem.
- Evaluate your tableau.

Teachers' note Explain the difference between a tableau and a play. A tableau presents one scene, rather than a story. The poem 'City Jungle' presents a tableau, which the children can enact. They should reread the poem and explore ways of enacting each image using body movements and facial expressions but no words. One child could read the poem aloud as they perform.

100% New Developing Literacy Understanding and Responding to Texts: Ages 10–11 © A & C BLACK

Mushrooms: 1

- **What kind of living beings are the mushrooms** | personified | **as?**
- **Circle the words.**
- **Link them to the poem.**
- **Explain your answers.**

Mushrooms

Overnight, very
Whitely, discreetly,
Very quietly

Our toes, our noses
Take hold on the loam,
Acquire the air.

Nobody sees us,
Stops us, betrays us;
The small grains make room.

Soft fists insist on
Heaving the needles,
The leafy bedding,

Even the paving.
Our hammers, our rams,
Earless and eyeless,

Perfectly voiceless,
Widen the crannies,
Shoulder through holes. We

Diet on water,
On crumbs of shadow,
Bland-mannered, asking

Little or nothing.
So many of us!
So many of us!

We are shelves, we are
Tables, we are meek,
We are edible,

Nudgers and shovers
In spite of ourselves.
Our kind multiplies:

We shall by morning
Inherit the earth.
Our foot's in the door.

Sylvia Plath

noisy   (quiet)

*because the poet uses the words
'discreetly' and 'very quietly' and
this gives a stealthy picture*

friendly   hostile

_____

_____

_____

powerful   weak

_____

_____

_____

welcoming   threatening

_____

_____

_____

NOW TRY THIS!

- **What sort of group of people do the mushrooms remind you of?**
- **Write a description and explain it.**

Teachers' note Give the children time to talk about the scene the poem conjures up. Ask them what the mushrooms are like. What is the atmosphere like? Focus on specific words and phrases that personify the mushrooms to create this atmosphere: the menacing effect of *earless* and *eyeless* and the quiet power of *shoulder through holes, soft fists insist* and *our hammers, our rams.*

**100% New Developing Literacy
Understanding and Responding
to Texts: Ages 10–11**
© A & C BLACK

Mushrooms: 2

• **Plan a story based on the poem 'Mushrooms'.**

Characters

Main

Other

Setting

What characters are the mushrooms?

Opening

Conflict

Beginning

What kind of conflict could come from the mushrooms?

Build-up

Climax

Resolution

Teachers' note Ask the children what kind of story the poem 'Mushrooms' suggests. Ask them when the action takes place and how people might respond when they wake up in the morning. What might they see? The children could enact this in their groups and explore the actions of the mushrooms and the responses of people.

100% New Developing Literacy Understanding and Responding to Texts: Ages 10–11 © A & C BLACK

Personify this

- [Personify] the garden items.
- **Write some words and phrases for a scary** [atmosphere].

Use precise nouns, strong verbs and powerful adjectives.

 the rake   <u>sharp teeth</u>

 a hosepipe   _____

 a fork   _____

 the shed   _____

 brambles   <u>tear at your flesh</u>

 a wheelbarrow   _____

 canes   <u>splinter into lethal shards</u>

 a spade   _____

Useful words

cling
creep
echo
eyes
glide
howl
mouth
rasp
rasping
rattle
shadow
sharp
shiver
shout
spiky
steely
tearing
teeth
throat
whine

NOW TRY THIS!

- **Write your ideas for a scary poem about the garden.**

Think of other words too.

100% New Developing Literacy Understanding and Responding to Texts: Ages 10–11
© A & C BLACK

Cynddylan before and after

- **Read the poem.**
- **Talk to your partner about how the tractor changed Cynddylan.**
- **On the back of this sheet, create a 'Before and After' chart.**
- **Write your ideas on the chart.**

Think about the connotations of 'yoked', 'proudly', 'as a great man should' and 'his nerves of metal and his blood oil'.

Cynddylan on a tractor

Ah, you should see Cynddylan on a tractor.

Gone the old look that yoked him to the soil;

He's a new man now, part of the machine,

His nerves of metal and his blood oil.

The clutch curses, but the gears obey

His least bidding, and lo, he's away

Out of the farmyard, scattering hens.

Riding to work now as a great man should,

He is the knight at arms breaking the fields'

Mirror of silence, emptying the wood

Of foxes and squirrels and bright jays.

The sun comes over the tall trees

Kindling all the hedges, but not for him

Who runs his engine on a different fuel.

And all the birds are singing, bills wide in vain,

As Cynddylan passes proudly up the lane.

R. S. Thomas

NOW TRY THIS!

- **How does the poet feel about the changes?**
- **List the words and phrases from the poem that tell you this.**

Teachers' note Ask the children about the image they have of Cynddylan. How does he feel driving the tractor? Does the poet think the tractor is a good thing? (Ask why he begins with *Ah.*) The children could look for images of power but also of the man being taken over by the machine. They could share their ideas about how the poet expresses feelings.

100% New Developing Literacy Understanding and Responding to Texts: Ages 10–11 © A & C BLACK

What's the issue?

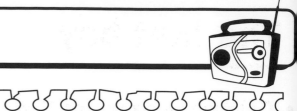

- **What is the poem about?**
- **What is its** message **?**
- **How does it make you feel?**

_____

_____

> **Take One Home for the Kiddies**
>
> On shallow straw, in shadeless glass,
> Huddled by empty bowls, they sleep:
> No dark, no dam, no earth, no grass –
> *Mam, get us one of them to keep.*
>
> Living toys are something novel,
> But it soon wears off somehow.
> Fetch the shoebox, fetch the shovel –
> *Mam, we're playing funerals now.*
>
> Philip Larkin

- **What is the mood of the first verse?** _____
- **List the** negative **words and phrases that communicate this.**

_____

_____

- **Reread the lines in italics.**
- **How does their mood contrast with the rest?** _____

_____

_____

- **Explain why the poet uses this contrast.**

> Think about the message of the poem.

_____

_____

NOW TRY THIS!

- **Collect information and stories connected with this issue.**
- **Write your thoughts about it.**

> Think of powerful words and phrases. Use contrast.

Teachers' note The children could read the poem in groups and discuss what they think it is about and what the poet is saying. They can then explore the ways in which the poet expresses his thoughts and feelings: through the use of negative words and phrases and contrast to express the way in which living things suffer when treated as playthings.

100% New Developing Literacy Understanding and Responding to Texts: Ages 10–11 © A & C BLACK

The hurt boy

- Colour the six words that best describe the boy's feelings at different points in the poem.
- Link them to the parts that express these feelings.

The Hurt Boy and the Birds

comfort

sorrow

The hurt boy talked to the birds
and fed them the crumbs of his heart.

It was not easy to find the words
for secrets he hid under his skin.
The hurt boy spoke of a bully's fist
that made his face a bruised moon –
his spectacles stamped to ruin.

hope

fear

It was not easy to find the words
for things that nightly hissed
as if his pillow was a hideaway for creepy-crawlies –
the note sent to the girl he fancied
held high in mockery.

loneliness

hurt

But the hurt boy talked to the birds
and their feathers gave him welcome –

Their wings taught him new ways to become.

misery

pain

John Agard

humiliation

NOW TRY THIS!

- What images does the poet use to communicate the boy's feelings?

Teachers' note Ask the children how they feel when they read this poem and what makes them feel like this. For a more challenging activity mask the words in the boxes and ask the children to identify powerful imagery and language that express the boy's feelings and use dictionaries and thesauruses to find the words that best describe them: for example, looking for alternatives for *sad*, *unhappy*, *hurt*.

100% New Developing Literacy Understanding and Responding to Texts: Ages 10–11 © A & C BLACK

Poems on an issue

- What do different poets say about destroying the natural world?
- How do they say it?
- Make notes on the chart.

Title	Poet	Message	Mood	How the poet communicates the message and mood

Think about imagery, metaphor, connotations of words, comparison, contrast, rhyme, rhythm, alliteration, onomatopoeia.

NOW TRY THIS!

- Plan a presentation about this ⬚issue⬚.
- Collect information. Use words from the poems.

Work in a group.

Teachers' note To prepare for this activity it is useful to have available a large collection of poems on the chosen issue (see *Notes on the activities,* page 12). Ask the children to look for powerful language that communicates the poet's feelings and thoughts about the issue.

100% New Developing Literacy Understanding and Responding to Texts: Ages 10–11
© A & C BLACK